BASKETBALL

TERENCE O'RORKE

Wayland

Go For Sport!
Basketball
Cricket
Fishing
Gymnastics
Judo
Karate
Rugby
Soccer

Cover: Michael Jordan of the Chicago Bulls – the biggest star of the NBA.

Picture acknowledgements
The publisher would like to thank Allsport for the pictures used in this book. Photographers: Howard Boylen 44; Tim Defrisco 5,7,21,26,31,35; Tony Duffy 12; Jim Gund 19 (bottom), 37; Ken Levine 16,29,38; Richard Martin 42; Gray Mortimer 9; Joe Patronite 10,18,20; Mike Powell 22,27,32 (top),33,41; D. Strohmeyer 25. The artwork is by Jo Dennis (Indent).

Series editor: James Kerr
Designer: Malcolm Walker

First published in 1993 by
Wayland (Publishers) Limited,
61 Western Road,
Hove, East Sussex, BN3 1JD

British Library Cataloguing in Publication Data
O'Rorke, Terence
  Basketball - (Go for Sport! Series)
  I. Title II. Series
  796.323

ISBN 0-7502-0663-2

Typeset by Kudos Editorial and Design Services
Printed and bound in Italy by G.Canale and C.S.p.A.

Contents

INTRODUCTION

Basketball is one of the most popular team sports in the world among men and women. It is played by an estimated 275 million people in every corner of the globe, and appeals to people of all ages and sizes. What's more, you do not need to be tall to play. It requires skill, speed, judgement, fitness and intelligence, and therefore has something for everyone. The rules ensure that it is an attacking game, and it is fast, exciting and very rewarding for both players and spectators.

The natural thing to do with a ball is to bounce it, throw it or catch it, and these are the basic skills of basketball. Although it is usually played indoors, it can also be played outside. The minimum requirements for a game are some flat ground, a basketball ring and a ball.

In countries with warm climates, it is common to see people playing in back gardens and driveways. Most American households have baskets attached to their garages. Basketball can be played with as many as ten players per side, or with just one-a-side. You can also play on your own, as many skills can be practised hour after hour without another person. The game is played at all levels – in schools, colleges and clubs, or just between friends in the park. In some countries, it is a multimillion dollar business played by some of the world's finest athletes, as well as being one of the most popular sports in the Olympic Games.

With the help of this book players should be able to grasp the fundamental skills of basketball and the teamwork involved. There are tips for the more advanced player on how to keep these skills up to scratch. No matter how good a player you are, if the basics are rusty then the rest of your game will suffer.

Spectacular slam dunks like this are what make basketball one of the most popular sports in the world.

HISTORY AND DEVELOPMENT

Basketball is the only major world sport to have originated in the USA. During the particularly cold winter of 1891, students at the International YMCA Training School in Massachusetts became tired of having gymnastics as their only indoor athletic activity. American football and baseball could not be played because the ground was too hard. Their PE instructor, Dr James Naismith, devised a game that they could play as an alternative to gymnastics. It had to be fast, skilful and fun, while at the same time non-contact. He took a soccer ball and hung a basket at each end of the gym. He then divided his class into two teams, and made the object of the game to throw the ball into the basket. The game caught on very quickly, and in 1893 Dr Naismith drew up a list of rules.

Because it is a non-contact game, basketball was originally more popular with women than men. In fact, the first US college match was played between young women from the University of California and Stanford in 1896. However, it wasn't long before men too began to play seriously. In 1901 the YMCA set up the first college basketball league, the Eastern Intercollegiate League. In 1908 the National Collegiate Athletics Association (NCAA) became the governing body of college basketball. For the next twenty-five years the sport was dominated by college teams. More and more leagues were formed and games were played before the public in major exhibition arenas.

In the 1930s the sport began to gain worldwide recognition for two reasons. Firstly, the Fédération Internationale de Basketball Amateur (FIBA) was formed in 1932 to govern the international game. Secondly, basketball became an Olympic sport in 1936. The gold medal was won by the USA, but more importantly, twenty-two teams took part in the competition. Basketball has been included in every Olympic Games since. Early on, the USA dominated the Olympic competition, winning seven successive titles, with the USSR, Brazil, Cuba and Yugoslavia regularly contesting the other medal places. But in 1972 US domination ended, after a series of controversial decisions enabled the USSR to win the final 51-50.

The USA has had professional

basketball since the turn of the century. However, it was overshadowed by the college game until 1946 when the Basketball Association of America was founded. In 1949 this organization joined with an older Midwestern body to form the National Basketball Association (NBA), and the pro game went from strength to strength.

There are a number of professional players who have helped make basketball one of America's top sports. Bob Cousy, Bill Russell, Wilt Chamberlain and Kareem Abdul-Jabbar are just a few. Cousy, only 1.85 m (6 ft 1 in) tall, had to rely on his superb dribbling and handling skills in an age when the game was already dominated by giants. He perfected the 'behind-the-back' dribble and when he was joined by Bill Russell – 2 m (6 ft 9 in) tall – at the Boston Celtics, the team went on to win nine NBA Championships in a row.

Standing 2.1 m (7 ft) tall, Wilt Chamberlain was one of the tallest players of his day. He held several

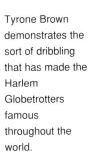

Tyrone Brown demonstrates the sort of dribbling that has made the Harlem Globetrotters famous throughout the world.

scoring records, averaging a remarkable 50 points per game in one season. He was succeeded by Kareem Abdul-Jabbar, another giant of a man. Using his 2.2 m (7 ft 4 in) frame to the full, Kareem was regarded as the greatest offensive player of his era and was voted the NBA's Most Valuable Player two seasons running.

Some credit for the growth of the sport should also go to the famous Harlem Globetrotters. Formed by Abe Saperstein in 1927, the all-African-American team started by playing exhibition matches around the USA. They perfected their very own circus-brand of basketball and though they have never been part of a league, they have all been professional players. As their reputation spread they travelled further afield, and have entertained crowds with their magical skills all over the world.

Today, the professional game in the USA is still dominated by star players. Michael Jordan of the Chicago Bulls, Karl Malone of Utah Jazz, Larry Bird of the Boston Celtics and Charles Barkley of the Philadelphia 76ers are just a few of the players who continue to thrill the crowds and push attendances to an all-time high.

At the 1992 Barcelona Olympics these great players were able to play together and represent their country for the first time. At previous Games, players from the NBA were not selected because of their professional status. The US side of 1992 was aptly named the 'Dream Team' and was described as the greatest basketball side ever to be assembled. Not surprisingly, they had little difficulty in sweeping aside all opposition on their way to the gold medal, with the likes of Michael Jordan and Magic Johnson proving too powerful for the opposition.

Basketball continues to grow in popularity, both as a professional sport and at the amateur level. There are now over 182 members of FIBA from all over the world. In the UK 440,000 players are registered, and the top professional sides can now take on the best teams in Europe. Australia and New Zealand have amateur and professional leagues, and as current Polynesian champions, Australia competed in the last Olympic Games.

The women's game also goes from

Suzanne McConnell in action for the US Olympic team.

the tallest woman ever to win an Olympic gold, but also the heaviest, weighing 129 kg (284 lbs). Women's basketball also thrives in Italy, Germany and Spain.

With slight alterations to the rules and equipment, the game has also become very popular amongst physically disadvantaged people. Like basketball, wheelchair basketball originated in the USA. Injured soldiers returning from the Second World War in 1945 were determined to enjoy one of the world's most popular sports, and therefore decided to play in wheelchairs.

By the 1950s, Stoke Mandeville Hospital in England had begun to use the game as a rehabilitation exercise for people with spinal injuries, and the game gradually took off in Britain. With the development of special wheelchairs to give extra speed and mobility, the game became more and more popular. It is the only team sport for wheelchair users. All sorts of people play the game, including paraplegics, amputees and people with spina bifida. In Britain alone, there are forty wheelchair basketball teams, with an estimated 400 players competing in the national league.

strength to strength. There are an estimated 40 million players worldwide, and women's world championships have been held since 1953. Women's basketball was introduced to the Olympics in 1976, and was dominated by the USSR. They were helped by their outstanding rebound player, Iuliana Semenova. At 2.1m (7 ft 1 in) tall, she is not only

ABOUT THE GAME

The objectives in basketball are simple. Each team must try and get the ball into the opposition's net as many times as possible by dribbling, passing and shooting, using only their hands. There are ten players on each side, though only five are allowed on court at any one time.

The court and equipment

Indoor and outdoor surfaces have to be hard and smooth, allowing the ball to bounce evenly and the players to move freely.

The ball: Balls are made of either leather, rubber or cheaper artificial materials. They should weigh 0.56-0.62 kg, have a circumference of about 0.76 m, and a diameter of 0.22 m. They are inflated to a degree that makes them bounce back about 1.25 m when dropped from a height of 1.80 m.

The court: The recommended dimensions of the court are 26 m in length and 14 m in width. These can vary depending on what country you are playing in, and at what level. Some courts will measure 28 m by 15 m.

The basket and backboard: The basket hangs from a solid metal ring, which is attached to the backboard. It has a diameter of 0.45 m and is 3.05 m from the surface of the court. The backboard measures 1.8 m by

You might think about wearing knee-pads, like Patrick Ewing of the New York Knicks.

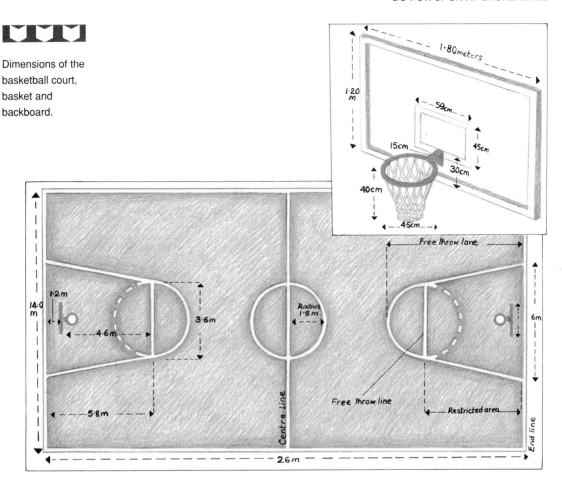

Dimensions of the basketball court, basket and backboard.

1.2 m, and is 1.2 m in from the end line. A rectangle is painted on to the backboard, with the bottom line level with the top of the net. The lowest edge of the backboard should be 2.75 m above the court, and for safety reasons, the supports should be at least 1 m behind the end line.

Clothing: As with most sports it is important to wear clothing that allows you to move freely. At first it is possible to play the game in a T-shirt, shorts, socks and training shoes. If you want to take the sport more seriously, then you should buy a pair of basketball boots. As you know, basketball requires a good deal of jumping, stopping and sharp turning, which puts a lot of stress on your ankle joints. Basketball boots are padded and come up above the ankle, giving added protection and a firm grip on the court. Some players wear two pairs of socks to help avoid blisters.

ORDER OF PLAY

Jump ball

Each half is started with a jump ball. The referee throws the ball in the air between a player from each team standing on either side of the centre line. They cannot go for the ball until it reaches its highest point. The team that secures the ball then has possession until they score a basket, make a foul, lose the ball to the other side, or let it go out of play.

A jump ball during the 1992 Olympic game between the USA and Czechoslovakia.

Time regulations

A game has two twenty-minute halves and a ten-minute break for half-time. The clock is started when the basketball is at its highest point during the jump ball, and the timekeeper stops the watch when the ball is out of play. This means exactly twenty minutes are played in each half. If the scores are level at the end of full-time, an extra five minutes are played to break the tie. If the game is still tied, another five minutes are played, and so on until there is a winner.

During a game there are a number of time limits you have to play to. These help the game to flow, and if a player breaks these rules, possession goes to the other side.

○ Thirty second rule – the attacking team has thirty seconds to take a shot.

○ Ten second rule – the attacking team has ten seconds to move the ball across the centre line. Once it has gone over this line it is not allowed to go into the back court during the attack.

○ Five second rule – a team has five seconds to bring the ball back into play (restart), and a player must pass, shoot or dribble within five seconds of receiving the ball.

○ Three second rule – a player on the attacking team is not allowed in the free throw area for longer than three seconds at a time.

During each half, a coach is allowed two time-outs, and signals to the scorer when he or she wants to take them. The clock will be stopped for exactly one minute, allowing the teams to make the necessary changes.

Scoring

P oints are awarded for three types of successful shot, and the referee will signal to the scorer how much a shot is worth:

○ Three point basket – when the player shoots from outside the three point line.

○ Two point basket – when the player shoots within the three point line.

○ One point basket – when the team is awarded a free throw after a foul has been committed by the opposition. Free throws must be taken from behind the free throw line.

Contact laws

Basketball was invented as a non-contact sport, but when there are up to ten players moving quickly in such a small area, a certain amount of contact is inevitable. It is sometimes difficult for referees to decide which player is at fault when contact occurs, so they will base their decision on the following principles:

○ Did the player try and avoid contact? Contact often occurs by mistake in basketball. If you accidently make contact with your opponent and he or she is not put at a disadvantage, you will not be penalized.

○ Did the player invade another player's 'personal space'? Each player has a 'personal space'. This is an imaginary area as wide as your shoulders, stretching from the floor to

Basketball is perhaps the most physical of non-contact sports.

the ceiling. If an opponent makes contact with you in your personal space, then he or she will be penalized.

There are occasions in a game when you are allowed to obstruct your opponent. If you manage to take up a defensive stance in the path of an opponent with the ball, then it is up to them to try and avoid you. If your opponent makes contact with your chest while dribbling the ball, then he or she will generally be at fault. If the contact occurs shoulder to shoulder, then most of the time the defender will be penalized. When opponents are not in possession, you must give them enough space to change direction or stop – this is usually about 1 m.

Fouls

There are three types of foul:

❍ Personal foul: This is called against a player who makes contact with his or her opponent. This will be by blocking, tripping, holding, pushing or charging with any part of the body. The other side are awarded a free throw. If a player commits five or more personal fouls, he or she is not allowed to take any further part in the game.

❍ Violation: This is an infringement that does not involve contact with an opponent. For example, taking more steps with the ball than is permitted. If a player commits a violation, the opposition are awarded a sideline throw.

❍ Technical foul: This can be committed by a player, substitute or coach, and involves actions which are not in the spirit of the game, for example swearing.

Free throws

Free throws are awarded against a team that breaks the rules. Each free throw is worth one point and the player must take the throw from behind the free throw line. The number of free throws awarded depends on the type of infringement. For example, if a player is fouled while shooting, he or she is awarded one free shot, plus two points if the original shot was successful. If the shot was missed, then the player is awarded two free throws if it was a two point shot or three free throws if it was a three point shot. For a technical foul, two free throws are awarded.

If a team commits seven fouls in one half, the one-and-one rule comes into effect. For every foul that the team then commits, the referee will award one throw, followed by another if it is successful.

Moving with the ball

When Dr Naismith first invented the game, a player wasn't allowed to move while in possession of the ball. Nowadays, however, this is allowed, but only when you are e i t h e r

Dan Marjerle of the Phoenix Suns demonstrates the balance and ball control needed to move the ball quickly down the court.

dribbling or pivoting (see chapters on skills). You can only play the ball with your hands, and are only allowed to bounce it using one hand at a time.

Positions

There are three positions in basketball:

○ Guard – the play-maker of the team. Guards are often smaller and faster than other players and should have excellent skills. They usually play at the rear of the attack, and should therefore be able to shoot from far out.

○ Centres – usually the tallest players in the side, they are positioned nearest the basket. They have to be excellent at scoring from close range and from rebounds.

○ Forwards – taller than guards and usually positioned between the sidelines and the restricted area. They are sometimes known as 'posts'.

Although you may be more suited to one position than another, each requires you to attack and defend, to pass, shoot and rebound. The positions are not as specialized as in other major team sports, for example soccer, American football or rugby.

The development
of special
wheelchairs,
giving extra speed
and mobility, has
made the game of
wheelchair
basketball fast
and exciting to
watch.

Wheelchair basketball

There are very few differences in the rules between basketball and wheelchair basketball. Wheelchair basketball starts with a tip-off, has similar time regulations and the system of scoring is the same.

The game differs in the way players dribble the ball. A player can either turn the wheels to push his or her chair and bounce the ball at the same time, or else place the ball on his or her lap and take one or two pushes of the wheelchair. The player must then bounce the ball, before pushing again.

Wheelchair basketball was also designed as a non-contact sport. The wheelchair is considered to be part of the player, and making contact when it could have been avoided counts as a foul. However, wheelchair basketball, like basketball, is a fast and furious game and players and officials are aware that contact is inevitable.

SKILLS 1

There are a variety of skills you need to master to be able to play basketball. This chapter explains the basic techniques you will have to learn, before moving on to some of the more complicated steps and movements.

The stance

It's important to get your stance right as it will improve your overall balance during play. At any moment, you may have to run, jump, twist or catch the ball, and if you are

A perfect defensive stance. The player in red has raised his arm to make it difficult for his opponent to pass.

not in the proper position for this, your reactions will be slow.

○ In offence – stand with your feet shoulder-width apart, one in front of the other, and with your knees slightly bent. Lean forward a little, and hold your arms out in front, with your hands level with your waist. You should feel comfortable in this position and ready to react to the demands of the game.

○ In defence – the aim is to make it difficult for your opponent to either shoot, pass or dribble round you. The defensive stance is similar to the offensive stance, except you have to alter the position of your arms, depending on what you think your opponent will do. For example, if you think he or she is going to pass over your head, keep one of your arms up.

Adopt a basketball stance in front of a mirror, just to make sure that you are standing correctly.

Ball handling

Once you are in the proper position you will be ready to handle the ball and hold, catch or pass it. Hold the ball with your fingers – try not to grab it with your whole hand. Use the fingertips of both hands, with your thumbs positioned behind the ball to increase your grip.

A basketball is larger and heavier than the balls used in other sports, and you should make sure you are comfortable handling it. There are a few simple drills you can practise to improve your confidence:

○ Circling your body – move the ball around your body at waist height by switching it from one hand to the other. One switch should occur behind you and the other in front of you. Circle your body ten times and repeat the exercise in the other direction. Once you have completed this, do it again but this time around your knees.

○ Figure-of-eight – stand with your knees slightly bent and your body leaning forward. Then pass the ball between your legs in a figure-of-eight, switching hands in the middle.

○ Overhead drop – drop the ball over your head, and catch it behind you before it hits the floor. You will have to move your arms at speed, and anticipate the fall of the ball.

Each of these drills should be completed without dropping the ball and, eventually, without looking at the ball. During a game you will not have time to look at your hands because you will have to follow the movements of your team-mates and the opposition. As you become more confident, repeat the drills at greater speed.

Passing and catching

Y ou must be able to deliver and receive a pass. There are a number of passes in basketball (see Skills 2 chapter) but the simplest one is the chest pass. With both hands, hold the ball in front of you at chest height, and with your elbows tucked in. Adopt the offensive stance (lean slightly forward with your knees bent) while looking at your target. Step forward and snap the ball to the other player. Remember to follow through with your arms, as this will help you transfer the ball at greater speed and with more accuracy. This type of pass is often used when there are no opposition players between you and the team-mate you are passing to. It is also used for the throw-in to restart play after the ball has gone out of bounds.

When catching, adopt the correct stance and concentrate on the following points:

❍   Keep your eyes on the ball.

❍   Make a target for the team-mate who is passing the ball to you.

❍   Once you have received a pass, make sure you have the ball under control.

❍   Prepare to either pass, dribble or shoot.

McConnell demonstrates a basic chest pass on the move. Note the extended arms in the follow-through.

Do not bounce the ball and catch it again once you have taken a pass, as this is ruled a dribble (see Skills 2 chapter). If you do this, you will have limited your options to passing or shooting.

SKILLS 2

As you become more confident and used to handling a basketball, you will want to improve your basic skills as well as learn new ones. The techniques discussed in this chapter will help you take your game one step further. You will be able to move with the ball, improvise your passing and develop your shooting.

Pivoting

Basketball is a game of almost non-stop action, most of which happens at each end of the court. As a player, you will be required to run up and down the court almost constantly. You will have to take passes on the run, and must be able to stop without a violation.

The pivot is a very useful skill to develop, and can be used to:

○ *Change the angle of attack – you can use it to make room for yourself to pass, shoot or dribble.*

○ *'Fake' to pass, shoot or dribble – if your opponent falls for the fake, you will have extra time to make your move.*

○ *Protect the ball from an opponent. Adopt the offensive stance as described earlier, but hold the ball in close to your chest with your elbows sticking out for protection.*

You must always pivot off the same foot until you release the ball. You may pivot as many times as you wish, but you must release the ball within five seconds.

The rules allow you to take one step in the process of stopping. Once you have stopped, you are then allowed to pivot off one foot, taking as many steps as you wish with the other foot, and in any direction. There are two ways of stopping in basketball – the stride stop and the jump stop.

○ **Stride stop:** This is the most common method and helps you stop while travelling at speed. There are two stages to the movement:

● Count one – as you receive the ball and your first foot lands, count 'one' to yourself. This is the foot you can pivot off and is generally your back foot.

● Count two – as your other foot lands, count 'two'. This is the foot you can move. It will generally be your front foot on stopping.

○ **Jump stop:** This is where both feet hit the ground at the same time. You are then allowed to use either foot to pivot off, but you must not change feet once you have chosen.

Dribbling

Dribbling is continuously bouncing the ball while moving or standing still, without letting it come to rest in one hand or both hands. Passing is the quickest way to move the ball, but you will not always have someone to pass to. If you decide not to pivot, you will have to dribble the ball until one of your team-mates is free to receive a pass or you are in position to shoot.

When dribbling, use your fingertips and thumb to control the ball, and

A young player dribbling the ball at speed. Notice how he is using just his fingertips and thumb to control the ball.

It is very important to be able to dribble with both hands. This will allow you to move down both sides of the court and protect the ball from defenders on either side.

your wrist to push the ball downwards. As the ball bounces back up, allow your hand and arm to rise with it slightly. Use your fingertips to cushion the force before pushing it down once more with your wrist. Try not to let the ball bounce above waist height.

There are two main ways of dribbling:

○ **Protected dribble:** You will need to use this when you are being closely guarded. Make sure your body is between the ball and the defender, keep your knees bent and use your free arm to shield the ball from your opponent. Try and keep the ball low, as this will make it more difficult for your opponent to steal it from you.

○ **Moving dribble:** This is also called the 'speed dribble' or 'high dribble'. It should be used when you are not under pressure, for example during a fast break out of defence. The ball should be bounced slightly higher and in front of you, so that you

can move on to it. You must also keep your head up at all times so that you can look out for a team-mate to pass to.

As you become more confident, you will be able to move the ball from one hand to the other. This is called the 'cross-over' dribble, and can be used to go round defenders. To switch from left to right, push the ball across the front of your body, when your left leg is in its most forward position. The bounce should not be too high, otherwise the defender can steal the ball. To cross-over from right to left, switch the ball when your right leg is forward.

When you have mastered these skills there are a number of more advanced dribbling techniques you can move on to.

○ **Behind-the-back dribble** – switching the ball from hand to hand by bouncing it behind your back.

○ **Between-the-legs dribble** – switching the ball from hand to hand by bouncing it between your legs.

○ **Spin dribble** – turning round 360 degrees while dribbling, keeping the body between the ball and the defender in order to give it maximum protection.

Passing:
Top left – the chest pass;
top right – the bounce pass;
bottom left – the overhead pass;
bottom right – the baseball pass.

Passing

In the last chapter you learnt how to throw a basic chest pass. However, there are times when this is not possible, and you will have

to pass the ball in another way.

○ **Bounce pass:** This is very useful when a defender is preventing you from throwing a chest pass. It is similar to the chest pass, using the same grip and arm movements, but

Close marking in basketball means passes must be made with pin-point accuracy.

Sherman Douglas
of Miami Heat
using the baseball
pass (see page
27).

the ball is released from waist height and bounced off the floor to your team-mate. The ball should bounce about three-quarters of the way between you both, so it reaches your team-mate on the way up. Bouncing the ball enables you to avoid the defender and it should reach your

Magic shows perfect technique in this set shot. Notice how the ball is sitting on the fingertips of his shooting hand while his other hand supports the ball from the side.

player at about hip height. You can throw it with one or both hands.

○ **Baseball pass:** This is used to throw the ball long distances and is similar to a throw made in baseball. Holding the ball in two hands, place one foot in front of the other, with the back foot firmly planted. When you are ready to throw, bring the ball back with the throwing arm and project it forward. As you do so, step forward with your front foot and follow through with your throwing arm.

○ **Overhead pass:** This is used to pass the ball over a defender and for reaching the tallest member of your side. Grip the ball in the same way as for a chest pass, but with your arms above your head. Throw the ball with your wrists and fingers, making sure it reaches your team-mate at head height. To put more power in the pass, take a step forward as you release the ball.

Shooting

E very member of a basketball team will be required to shoot during a game. There are a number of shots to learn, each of which will allow you to shoot under different

circumstances. Remember to use the backboard, as it is not always possible to shoot directly into the basket.

○ **The set shot:** This is the easiest shot to learn and should be used when an opponent is between you and the basket. There are a number of steps to follow:

● Adopt the correct stance for balance – feet facing the basket with knees slightly bent. Hold the ball with your fingers and thumbs at chest height, and look at the basket.

● Bring the ball up slowly until it rests on the fingertips of your shooting hand, with your wrist acting as a platform. Use your other hand to support the ball from the side.

● Straighten your shooting arm and legs, and at the same time snap your wrist, so that the ball rolls off your fingertips. This will give it slight backspin, which will take some of the speed off it when it hits the backboard.

● Follow through with your shooting arm until it is fully extended, as this will help your aim. Your wrist should be pointing downwards at the end of

The set shot.

Ken Norman of the LA Clippers executes a lay-up shot in a game with the LA Lakers (see page 30).

the shot – imagine you are trying to dip your hand into the basket.

○ **The free throw:** The free throw is more or less the same as the set shot. The only difference is that for the free throw your feet have to be positioned behind the free throw line. Most players follow a strict routine of bouncing the ball several times before shooting. This helps them relax and

The lay-up.

gives them a higher success rate. Nothing annoys a coach more than seeing one of his or her players miss a free throw!

○ **The lay-up:** This is performed when you are moving and close to the basket. There are a number of steps to follow:

● You begin the shooting action by taking two steps. Count 'one' on the first and 'two' on the second. As you take your second step, bend the knee and spring off the landed foot towards the basket.

● At the same time, raise your opposite knee and straighten the

30

Scottie Pippen – one of the stars of the NBA – shows how a jump shot can help to give you a clearer shot at the basket when there is a defender in the way.

shooting arm. Keep your body as upright as possible as this will give you more height and help you to get closer to the basket.

● Gently propel the ball towards the square on the backboard so that it drops back into the net.

Use this shot when you are attacking the basket from either side. When moving from the left, use your left arm to shoot, come off your right leg and raise the left knee. This will help you to protect the ball and gain more height in the jump. When moving from the right, simply reverse the technique.

○ **The jump shot:** This is useful when there is a defender between you and the basket. It is very similar to the set shot, but instead of just straightening your legs, spring upwards and release the ball at the top of your jump. This will help you rise above the defender giving you a clearer shot at the basket.

○ **The hook shot:** This is a modification of the lay-up and should be used when you are close to the basket. As you come off one leg, raise the other knee, and extend your shooting arm towards the basket. Flick the wrist when your arm is fully extended above you, so the ball drops into the basket.

○ **The slam dunk:** You won't be able to perform this shot until you are a little taller because you have to jump so high. It is the most spectacular shot and requires a player to jump to a height where his or her arms are above the level of the basket. The ball is then dunked into the basket using one or both hands. There is a

will have one of two aims:

○ In defence – to win the ball and gain possession. If you cannot win it cleanly, try and 'bat' it away so the opposition cannot score.

○ In offence – to tap the ball into the basket. This is called a 'tip-in' and you won't be able to perform this until you are a little taller.

Successful rebounding requires good anticipation and positioning. As a defender, you will normally be between your opponent and the basket. When the shot is taken you can obstruct your opponent's path to the basket. This is called 'blocking out' the opponent.

The hook shot.

slam dunk competition at the NBA All-Star Game. The winner is the player who takes-off furthest from the basket.

Rebounding

Roy Tarpley of the Dallas Mavericks reaches up for a rebound in a game with the Charlotte Hornets.

R ebounding is jumping for the ball after another player has missed a shot. It is a vital part of the game because shots are so often missed. Players going for a rebound

TEAMWORK

B asketball is all about teamwork at speed. To be able to fit into a team you will have to be able to perform the basic skills discussed earlier in the book. It helps to be a skilful individual player, but you must be aware that games are won through good teamwork, whether this is in defence or attack. Remember that teamwork comes first and individual play second.

Team defence

I n the Skills 1 chapter we saw how to defend against an individual attacker in possession of the ball by adopting the correct stance and using the arms and body to block his or her movements.

It is also important to defend against players who are not in possession. Every member of a

James Worthy of the Lakers looks around for a team-mate to pass to.

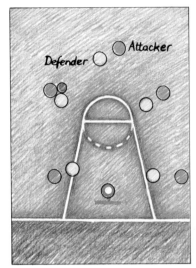
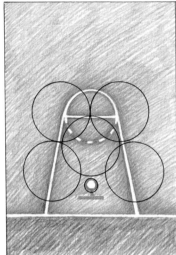
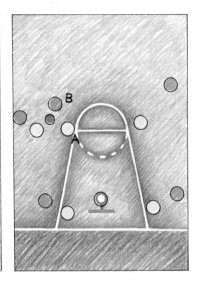

Team defence:
Left – one-to-one defence used half-court. Notice how each defender is between an opponent and the basket; middle – zone defence used half-court. Each defender protects an area around the key; right – 'box and one'. Four defenders mark zones around the key, with one player (A) continuously marking the opposition's best player (B).

basketball team has an important defensive role, and when you're not attacking, you should be back defending. There are two main styles of defence, and a team should be able to play both.

○ **One-to-one defence:** This is where each defender is responsible for marking an attacking player. In one-to-one defence, make sure you are between the basket and the player you are defending. Pressurize your attacker as soon as he or she receives the ball. This gives the attacker less time to decide what to do, and you could force an error.

One-to-one defence can be used in two ways:

● Half-court – this is one-to-one defence in the back court only. As attackers cross the centre line, each one is picked up by a defender.

● Full-court – sometimes your coach will think it necessary to move the one-to-one defence up to three-quarters of the court or the whole court. Coaches do this to put more pressure on the opposition, forcing them to make errors. 'Full-court' is also used by coaches to 'up the tempo', often when the team is ahead and there are only a few minutes left. Players are picked up as soon as the opposition has the ball. If the opposition are successful in moving the ball out of defence, remember to get back quickly to defend.

○ **Zone defence:** This is an

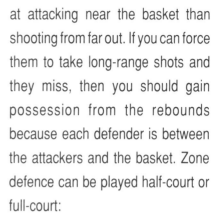

A perfect example of how to block an attempted shot.

alternative to one-to-one defence. Rather than defending against another player, you have to defend a specific area or zone. It is designed to protect the area around the key and is used against teams that are better at attacking near the basket than shooting from far out. If you can force them to take long-range shots and they miss, then you should gain possession from the rebounds because each defender is between the attackers and the basket. Zone defence can be played half-court or full-court:

● Half court – the simplest zone defence is the 2-1-2 formation. The two smallest players protect the front zones, the post player protects the middle, and the two tallest players play at the back. If you are nearest to the player in possession then you must pressurize him or her at all times. If the attack changes direction, be ready to move with it, but stay within your zone. When the opposition shoot, remember to block the player in your zone to prevent him or her from getting to the rebound.

● Full court – this is similar to full-court one-to-one defence, but each defender marks a zone instead of a player. Players adopt a 2-2-1 formation and aim to trap the ball in one of the zones. The front two players allow the throw-in and pressurize the opponents into taking the ball near the end line and dribbling down

Team offence:
Left – splitting the post. Player 1 passes to player 2 and follows the ball. Player 3 runs towards player 2. Defenders will find it difficult to mark players 1 and 3 because player 2 is screening them; *right* – screen. Player 1 passes to player 2 and then sets a screen on player 3. This makes it harder for the defence to mark player 3, who can then cut towards the basket and receive a pass from player 2.

the sidelines. When an attacker reaches an area where two zones overlap, two defenders can trap him or her. The other defenders should be ready to intercept any passes thrown from the trapped opponent.

You will have to learn both one-to-one and zone defence. Your coach could ask you to combine them during a game as this will make the team more flexible.

'Box and one' is a form of zone defence aimed at cancelling out the best player on the opposite team. It is achieved by putting a permanent marker on him or her. Four of the team will defend in zones with the fifth marking their best player. However, be careful when using this tactic as it can leave defences open. It is not as safe as the one-to-one or zone defences.

Team offence

Ideally, most teams would like to be able to break out of defence and set up a scoring chance before the opposition can get back into defensive positions. This is called a 'fast break', but it is not always possible. Every coach, therefore, will have an offensive pattern which he or she hopes will lead to an open shot every time the team has possession.

○ **Motion offence:** In this type of attack, the players are moving all the time. It involves fast, accurate passing which can break down one-to-one defences. The guard (the best ball-handler) will generally be at the centre of this attack. He or she is positioned slightly behind the forwards, who are to the left and right, around the front of the key. These players are

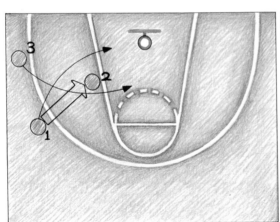

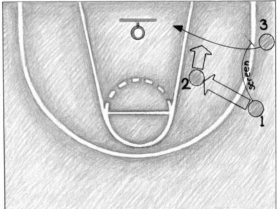

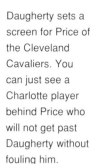

Daugherty sets a screen for Price of the Cleveland Cavaliers. You can just see a Charlotte player behind Price who will not get past Daugherty without fouling him.

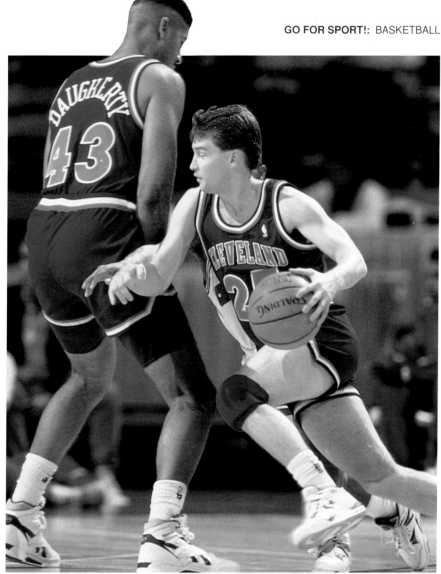

generally good at long range shooting. The two centres – the tallest players – are on either side of the basket. They make good targets and are the best at scoring from close range.

A good ploy in a motion offence is the 'screen'. This is when a player occupies some space on the court and prevents an opponent from following a team-mate. It requires lots of practice and there are a number of patterns involving screens. Here are a couple of simple ones:

● Screen and pass – player 1 passes to player 3, then sets a screen on player 2. Player 2 is then free to move into a position where he or she can receive a pass and shoot.

● Splitting the post – player 1 passes to player 2, and follows the ball. Player 3 then runs towards player 2, arriving just after player 1. Defenders will find it difficult to mark players 1 and 3, because player 2 is setting a screen for them. Player 2 can then pass to either player 1 or 3.

❍ **Zone offence:** This is used to try and break down a zone defence. Again, it is useful to try and set up screens. You should be on the move as much as possible, with lots of passing between the team. There are two main points to remember:

● Keep a distance between yourself and the other attacking players. This spreads the defence and creates more gaps.

● Try and get into positions between the defensive zones. This forces defenders out of their zones and leaves gaps for attackers.

❍ **Press offence:** This is used against a full-court one-to-one defence. After the opposition have scored, your players must position themselves quickly to receive the ball, and try and break down the one-to-one marking. The ball must be brought into play quickly and moved up the court as soon as possible.

Coaches and Referees

Coaches and referees are very important in basketball. Remember, the sport could not exist without them. Coaches have a major role to play, not only in training, but also during a game. Basketball is all about tactics and your coach will teach you these. He or she will tell you what tactics to use and when to change them. You must listen to the coach and do as he or she says. Basketball is a team game and if an individual thinks he or she knows more than the coach, then team spirit will suffer.

You should also respect referees. Accept their decisions as right, even if you think they have made a mistake. Referees have a difficult role to play, as the contact laws are not always easy to interpret. When ten players are running around a small court, some contact is inevitable. A referee must allow for this so the game can flow.

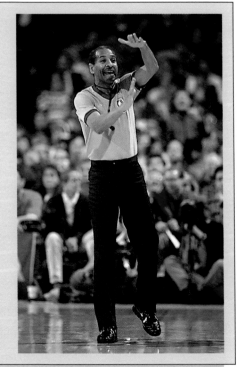

FITNESS AND TRAINING

Warming up before a game helps to prevent strains and injuries.

Warming up

Before a game or training session, you must warm up thoroughly. As you know, basketball requires the use of most of your muscles for jumping, running and twisting, and these muscles need to be stretched to avoid injury.

Most of the time your coach or captain will lead the warm up. But if you have to warm up on your own, there are a few simple exercises you can follow (see page 40). Basketball makes particular demands on your legs, arms, back, hips and ankles.

Try and stretch each muscle individually, and if you are recovering from an injury, spend a little more time on the affected area.

Jogging and skipping are also good ways of warming up. Jogging uses a variety of muscles, and skipping helps to make you light on your feet. Both are good for building up stamina.

It is important to warm down after a game or a hard work-out. Put on a tracksuit to avoid getting cold, and gently jog on the spot or 'loosen-off' to cool down, before showering.

Fitness

I f you want to improve at any sport, you must be fit. You are less likely to get injured and it will help you when you are learning difficult skills. These can only be mastered by practice and the fitter you are, the more you will be able to concentrate.

Basketball is a very fast game and you have to be fit to play it well. Games are often decided in the last few minutes and if you are too tired by this stage, then your opponents will obviously have an advantage. Your coach will have worked out a set of fitness drills, but here are a few simple exercises to help. Build up the length of time spent on each exercise.

○ Press-ups – remember to keep your body straight. These will help to strengthen your arms and wrists. If you can, try finger press-ups to strengthen the fingers.

To be a top basketball player like Charles Barkley of the 76ers, you have to be very fit.

❍ Skipping – this is good for strengthening leg and calf muscles. It also makes you more nimble on your feet, and builds up stamina.

❍ Shuttle runs – sprinting and jogging between a series of markers, with the distance increasing each time. This is good for speed work and stamina, and can be practised with or without a ball.

❍ Bench jumps – two-footed, sideways jumps over a low-level bench. This is good for leg and calf muscles, and helps build strength for jumping.

Good close, protected dribbling like this in a high pressure game situation is only achieved through hours of solitary practice.

Training

The beauty of basketball is that you can practise nearly all the skills on your own. If you have half an hour to spare at lunch-time or even ten minutes before supper, you can spend it polishing up your dribbling, shooting or passing. For some of the skills you don't even need a basket. Some flat ground, a wall and a ball are all you need to practise dribbling and passing. Here are a few simple training drills:

○ **Passing:** If you have a partner, you can practise all the passes you have learnt. Vary the distance between yourselves and the height at which you want to receive the pass. If you have two balls, pass these between you at the same time using different passes.

If you are on your own, practise passing against a wall. Again, vary the height and distance of your passes. Increase the speed to improve your strength and reactions and try not to drop the ball.

○ **Dribbling:** A low figure-of-eight dribble between your legs, changing hands in the middle (like in the ball handling exercise), is good for practising fingertip control. Do twenty in one direction and then twenty in the other.

Use the whole of the flat ground for high-dribble practice. If you have some markers, dribble round them, first with one hand and then with the other. Vary your speed and practise a changeover in the middle. Concentrate on improving your weaker side, otherwise opponents will spot your weakness and play to it.

○ **Shooting:** Start off practising the set shot from around the key, using both hands. Try and concentrate as you shoot because during a game you cannot afford to be careless. Move back one metre and repeat the exercise. Do the same drill for the jump shot. For the lay-up, start on the centre line, run to the basket and shoot. Vary your speed and the hand you shoot with. Repeat the exercise using the whole length of the court. If you have a partner, throw and receive a pass before the shot. Again, practise with your weak hand.

Basketball can be enjoyed at all levels. If you wish to improve your game then you will have to practise regularly and stay fit. The more you

The high five and the low five originated in basketball but are now standard forms of friendly greeting. Keep the spirit of the game alive by playing seriously but fairly. Above all, enjoy the game.

put in to the sport, the more you will get out of it. Basketball has become one of the most popular sports in the world because it allows players to express individual skills, while at the same time putting a lot of emphasis on teamwork.

If you work at both aspects of your game then you will get a lot of satisfaction from it – there is nothing more pleasing than scoring from a well-worked move involving all of your team-mates. Be sporting at all times – don't gloat when you win a match, and remember to congratulate the opposition when you lose. The most important thing of all is to enjoy your game.

Glossary

Assist   A pass that leads to a successful shot.

Back court   The half of the court that your team is defending.

Bat   To knock the ball away from another player using the palm of your hand.

Boxing out   Defenders taking up a position to prevent attackers getting near the basket.

Charging foul   When an attacking player charges into a stationary defender.

Double foul   Two opposing players fouling each other at the same time, resulting in a jump ball.

Double team   Two defenders trapping one attacker.

Fake   Also known as a 'dummy' or 'feint'. Pretending to pass, shoot or dribble to fool your opponent. This helps to create time and room for yourself.

Free throw   A penalty shot awarded after a foul. It is taken from the free throw line.

Front court   The half of the court your team is attacking.

High post   Position near the top of the key furthest from the basket.

Inbound   Bringing the ball into play.

Jump ball   When two players jump for the ball to decide which team gains possession.

Key   The area around the basket marked out by lanes.

Low post   Position at the bottom end of the key near to the basket.

One-on-one   One attacker versus one defender.

One-to-one   Marking an opponent rather than a section of the court.

Playmaker   Another name for the guard.

Rebound   When the ball bounces back after a missed shot.

Screen   When one player moves into an area of the court to prevent an opponent marking a team-mate.

Strong side   The side of the key in which the attacking team have the ball.

Travelling   Moving with the ball but failing to bounce it correctly.

Weak side   The side of the key in which the attacking team doesn't have the ball.

Further information

Useful addresses

Amateur Basketball Association of USA
1750 East Boulder Street
Colorado Springs
CO 80909
USA

Australian Basketball Federation
1st Floor, 203 New South Head Road
Edgecliff 2027
NSW
Australia

Basketball Canada
1600 James Naismith Drive
Ste. 809
Gloucester
Ontario KIB 5N4
Canada

English Basketball Association
48 Bradford Road
Leeds LS28 6DF
England

Fédération Internationale de Basketball
 Amateur (FIBA)
Kistlerhofstrasse 168
W - 800 Munchen 70
Germany

Great Britain Wheelchair Basketball
 Association
116 Chadwell Heath Lane
Chadwell Heath
Romford
Essex RM6 4AE
England

National Basketball Association (NBA)
Olympic Tower
645 5th Avenue
New York
NY 910022
USA

New Zealand Basketball Federation
PO Box 19168
Avondale
Auckland 7
New Zealand

Further reading

Basketball Dribblers Manual and *Basketball Passers Manual* – YMCA USA (1984)
Basketball - The Skills of the Game by Paul Stimpson (Crowood Press, 1986)
Coaches Manual - the English Basketball Association (1985)
Know About Basketball by Chris Bunnett and Sean McSweeney (AA Publishing, 1990)
Play the Game - Basketball by David Titmuss (Ward Lock, 1989)
Step by Step Basketball Skills by Joe Whelton and Richard Taylor (Hamlyn, 1988)

Major competitions

International
○ *Olympic Games*
Held every four years.
Men: Twelve teams take part, with the host nation and gold medallist from the last world championships qualifying automatically. The remainder need to qualify through the five FIBA zones – Africa, Americas, Asia, Europe and Oceania.
Women: Eight teams take part, with the host nation and three best-placed teams from the last world championships qualifying automatically. The remaining four places go to the four best-placed teams from the World Olympic Qualifying Tournament for Women, organized by the five FIBA zones.

○ *World championships*
Held every four years.
Men: Sixteen teams take part. The host nation and the Olympic gold medallists gain automatic entry, and the remaining fourteen places are divided amongst the five zones of FIBA.
Women: Sixteen teams take part. The host nation gains automatic entry, with the other fifteen places divided amongst the five FIBA zones.

Club
○ *NBA (USA) Twenty-seven teams are divided into two conferences. The Eastern Conference is made up of the Atlantic Division and the Central Division, each of which has seven teams. The Western Conference is made up of the Midwest Division, with six teams, and the Pacific Division with seven teams. Sixteen teams qualify for the play-offs – the four divisional winners, plus the six teams from each conference with the best win-loss record. A knock-out competition from each conference decides which two teams play each other in the best-of-seven NBA Finals.*
○ *European Championships for Men's Clubs (ECM) – all European national champions.*
○ *European Cup for Men's Clubs (ECGM) – all European national cup winners.*
○ *European Cup Radivoj Korac (ECK) – maximum of four clubs from each national federation.*
○ *European Cup for Women's Champion Clubs – all European national champions.*
○ *European Cup Liliana Ronchetti (ECLR) – maximum of four clubs from each national federation.*

Index

Numbers in **bold** refer to captions.